What Did Robot Want?

🦷 Dominie Press, Inc.

Robot could not read well.
He needed new batteries.

Robot wanted
some new batteries.
But he could only read "b."

Robot saw a "b" word. He said, "Please give me two of those."

The man gave Robot
two bananas.

Robot saw another "b" word.
He said, "Please give me
two of those."

bread

The woman gave Robot
two loaves of bread.

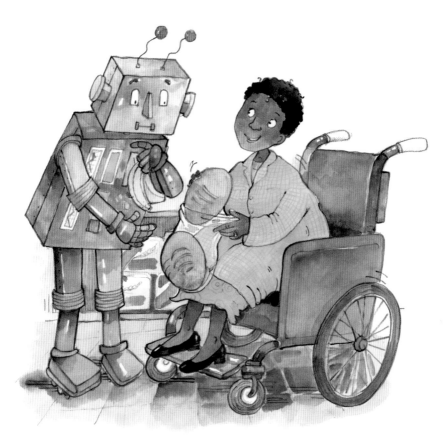

Robot saw another "b" word.
He said, "Please give me
two of those."

books

The man gave Robot two books.

"Oh dear!" said Robot.
"I don't want bananas.
I don't want bread.
I don't want books.
I want b- b- b- b- b."

Robot tried again.

Robot saw another "b" word.
He said, "Please give me
two of those."

bags

The woman gave Robot two bags.

"Oh dear!" said Robot.
"I don't want bananas.
I don't want bread.
I don't want books.
I don't want bags.
I want b- b- b- b- b."

"Wait!" called a girl.
"I know what you want."

"You want batteries,"
said the girl.